SOLO GUITAR • STANDARD NOTATION AND TAB

SUNDAY SOLOS
for GUITAR

20 FINGERPICKING ARRANGEMENTS
FOR BLENDED WORSHIP

ISBN 978-1-4584-2464-8

HAL•LEONARD®
CORPORATION

7777 W. BLUEMOUND RD. P.O. BOX 13819 MILWAUKEE, WI 53213

Visit Hal Leonard Online at
www.halleonard.com

INTRODUCTION TO FINGERSTYLE GUITAR

Fingerstyle (a.k.a. fingerpicking) is a guitar technique that means you literally pick the strings with your right-hand fingers and thumb. This contrasts with the conventional technique of strumming and playing single notes with a pick (a.k.a. flatpicking). For fingerpicking, you can use any type of guitar: acoustic steel-string, nylon-string classical, or electric.

THE RIGHT HAND

The most common right-hand position is shown here.

Use a high wrist; arch your palm as if you were holding a ping-pong ball. Keep the thumb outside and away from the fingers, and let the fingers do the work rather than lifting your whole hand.

The thumb generally plucks the bottom strings with downstrokes on the left side of the thumb and thumbnail. The other fingers pluck the higher strings using upstrokes with the fleshy tip of the fingers and fingernails. The thumb and fingers should pluck one string per stroke and not brush over several strings.

Another picking option you may choose to use is called hybrid picking (a.k.a. plectrum-style fingerpicking). Here, the pick is usually held between the thumb and first finger, and the three remaining fingers are assigned to pluck the higher strings.

THE LEFT HAND

The left-hand fingers are numbered 1 through 4.

Be sure to keep your fingers arched, with each joint bent; if they flatten out across the strings, they will deaden the sound when you fingerpick. As a general rule, let the strings ring as long as possible when playing fingerstyle.

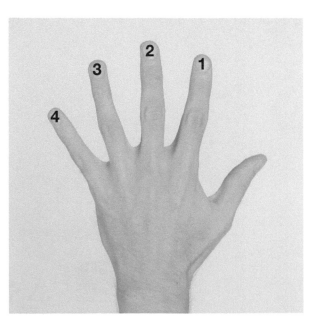

CONTENTS

Amazed

Words and Music by Jared Anderson

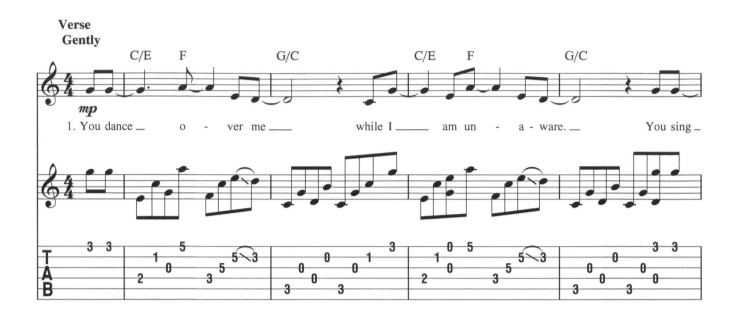

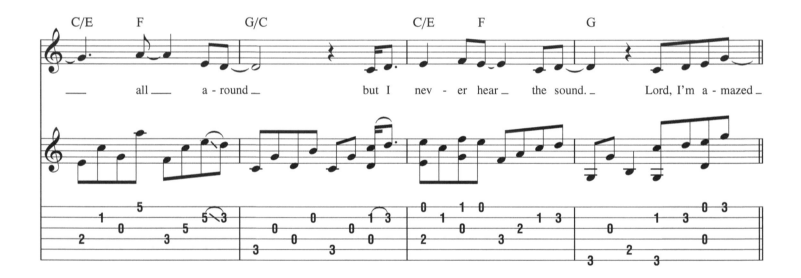

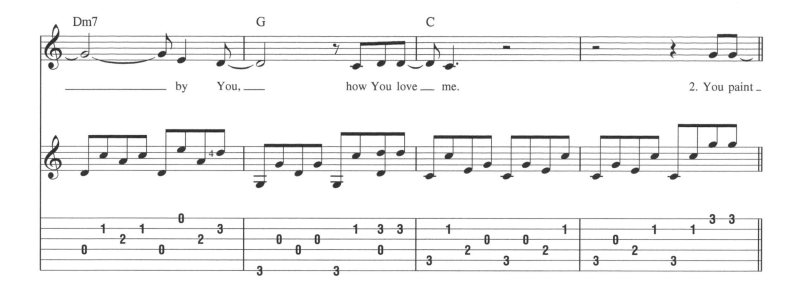

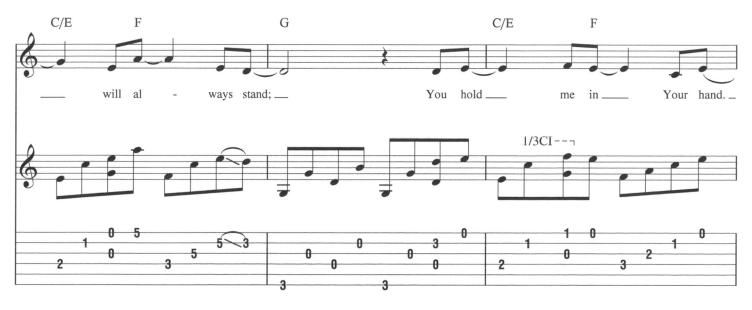

5

Chorus

Lord, I'm a - mazed _____ by You. ___ Lord, I'm a - mazed

_____ by You. ___ Lord, I'm a - mazed _____ by You, _

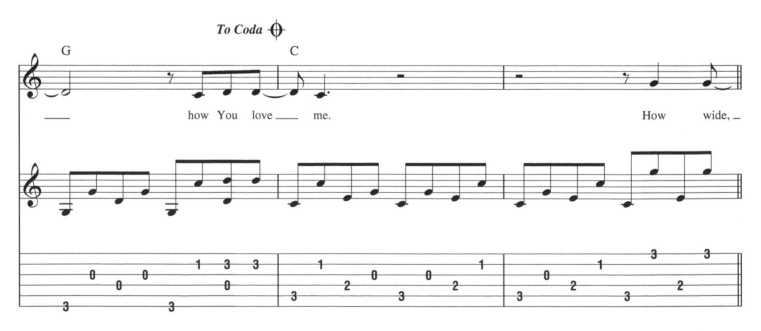

To Coda

how You love ___ me. How wide, _

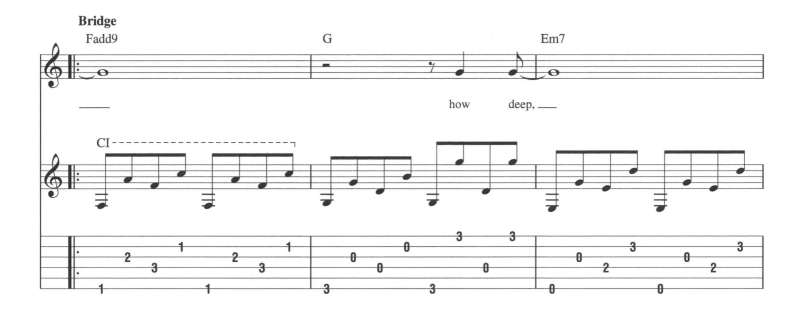

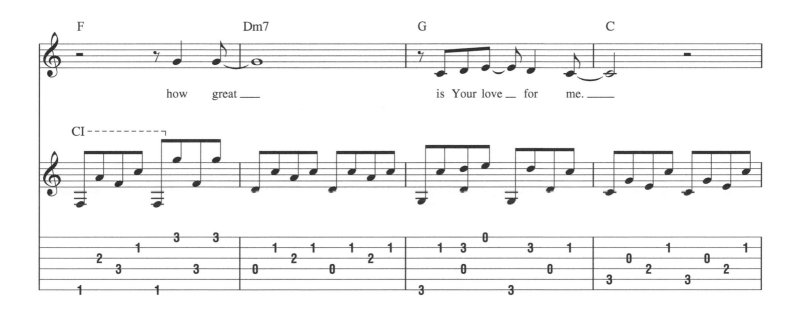

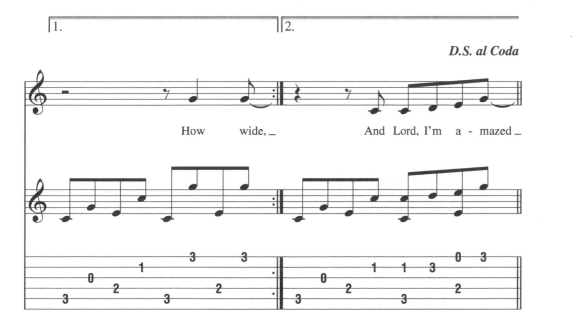

Blessed Assurance

Lyrics by Fanny J. Crosby
Music by Phoebe Palmer Knapp

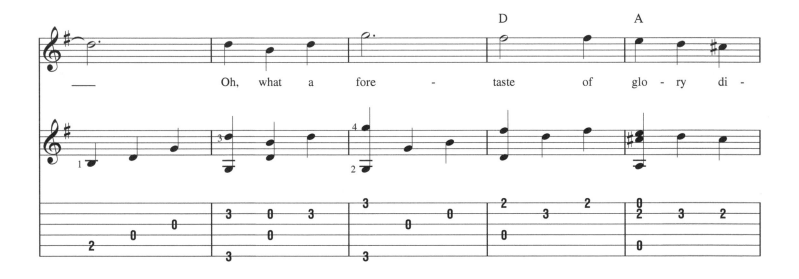

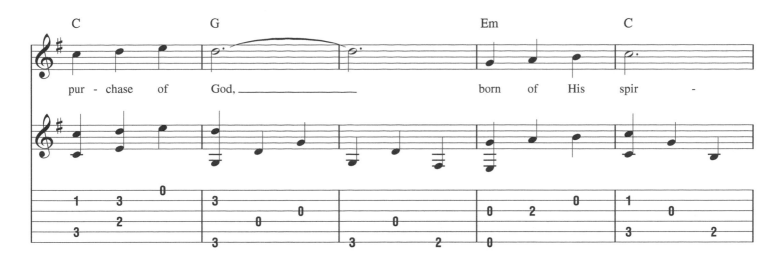

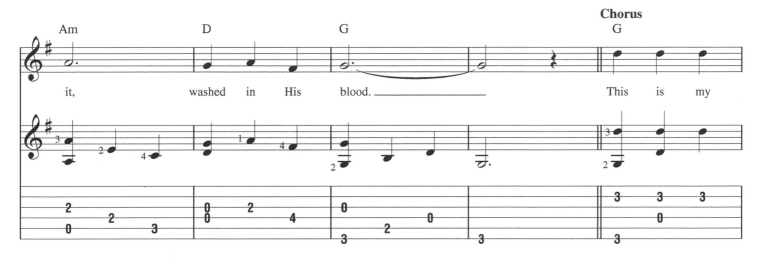

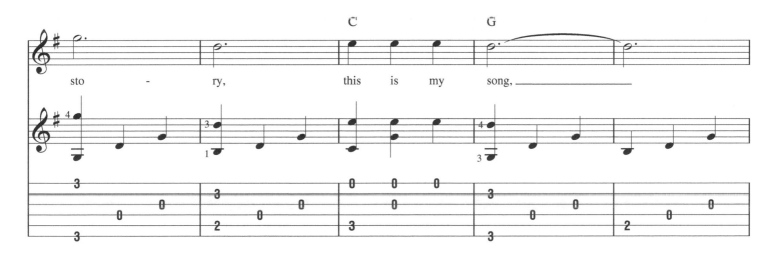

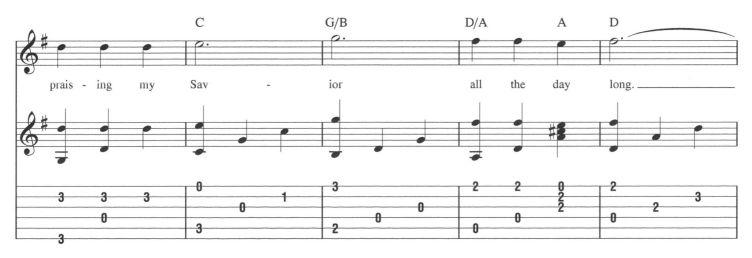

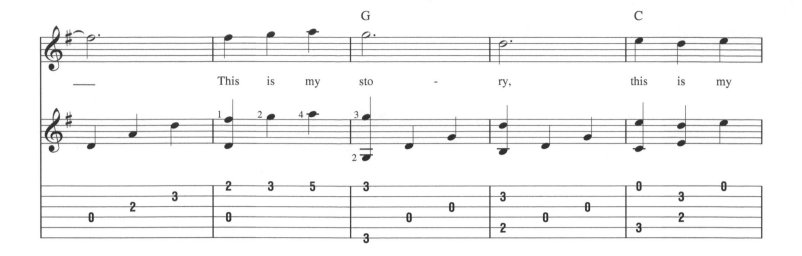

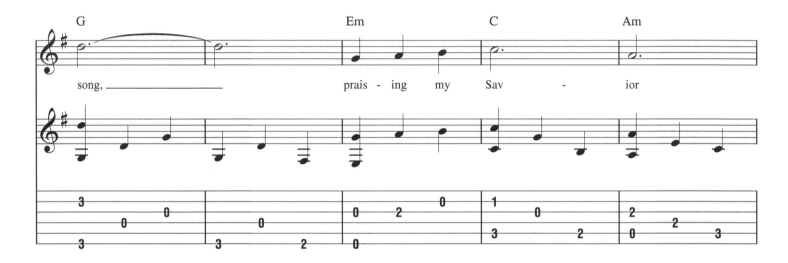

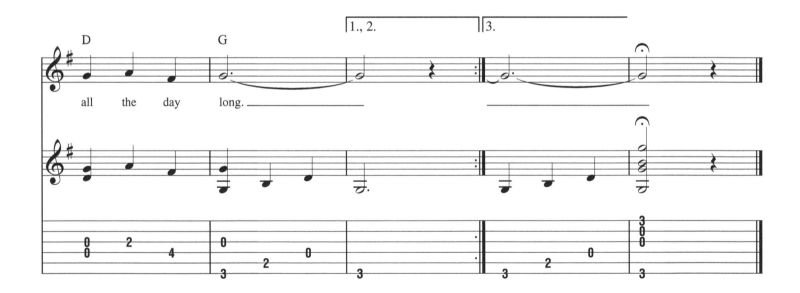

Additional Lyrics

2. Perfect submission, perfect delight,
   Visions of rapture now burst on my sight;
   Angels descending, bring from above
   Echoes of mercy, whispers of love.

3. Perfect submission, all is at rest.
   I in my Savior am happy and blest,
   Watching and waiting, looking above,
   Filled with His goodness, lost in His love.

Great Is Thy Faithfulness

Words by Thomas O. Chisholm
Music by William M. Runyan

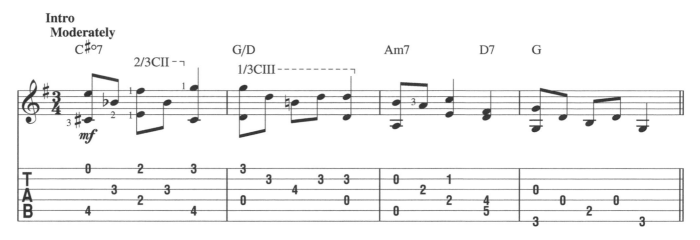

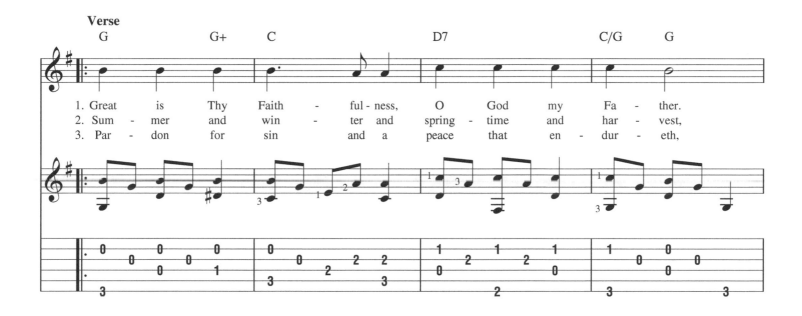

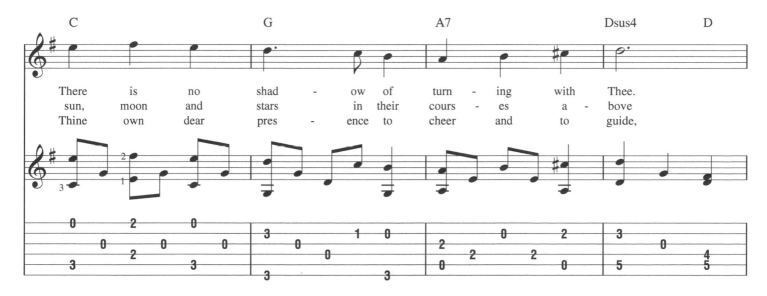

Thou chang - est not, Thy com - pas - sions they fail not,
join with all na - ture in man - i - fold wit - ness
strength for to - day and bright hope for to - mor - row,

as Thou hast been Thou for - ev - er will be.
to Thy great faith - ful - ness, mer - cy and love.
bless - ings all mine, with ten thou - sand be - side!

Chorus

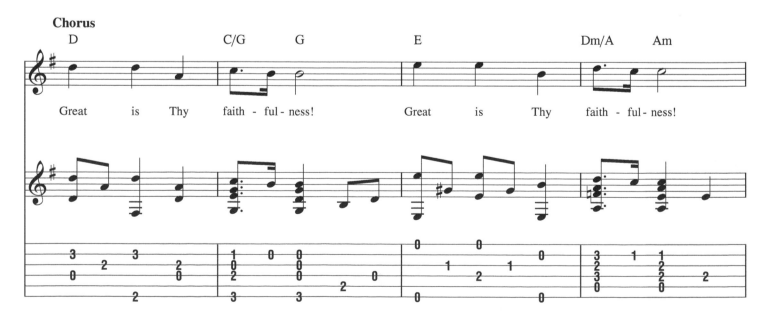

Great is Thy faith - ful - ness! Great is Thy faith - ful - ness!

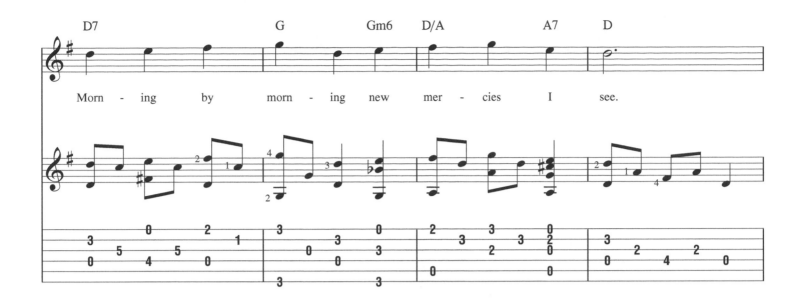

Morn - ing by morn - ing new mer - cies I see.

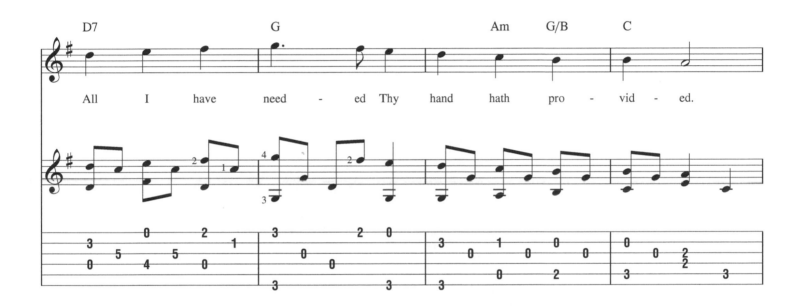

All I have need - ed Thy hand hath pro - vid - ed.

Great is Thy faith - ful - ness, Lord un - to me! me!

Give Thanks

Words and Music by Henry Smith

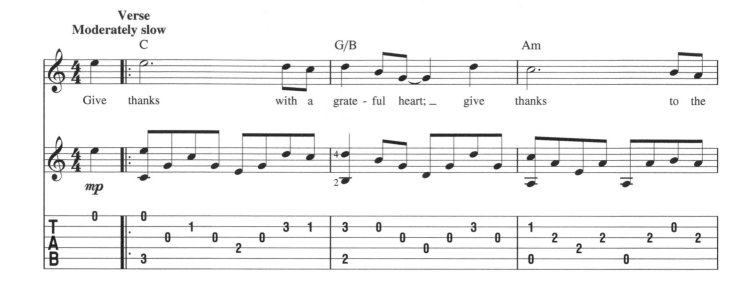

Chorus

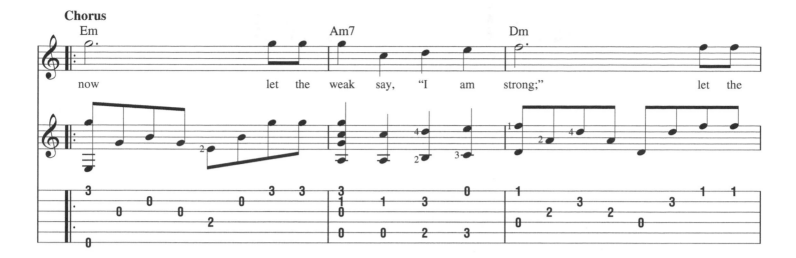

now   let the weak say, "I am strong;"   let the

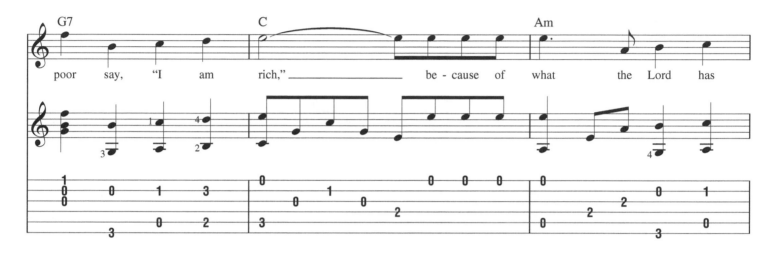

poor say, "I am rich," _____ be - cause of what the Lord has

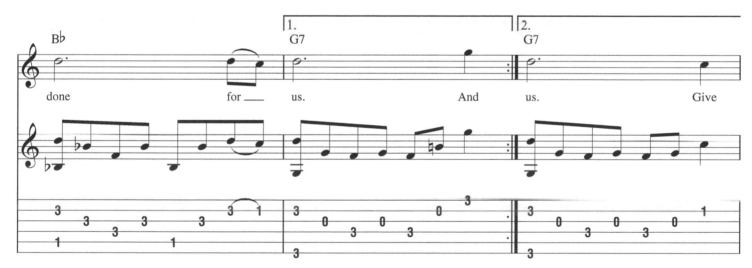

done   for __ us.   And   us.   Give

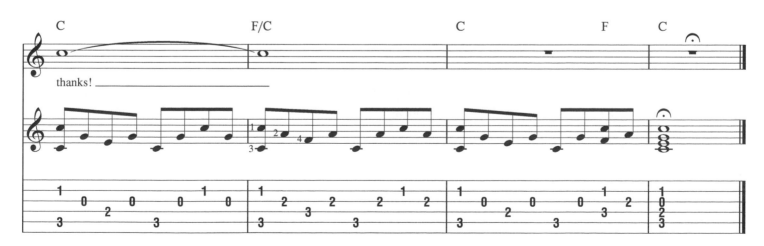

thanks! _____

Here I Am to Worship

Words and Music by Tim Hughes

*T = Thumb on 6th string

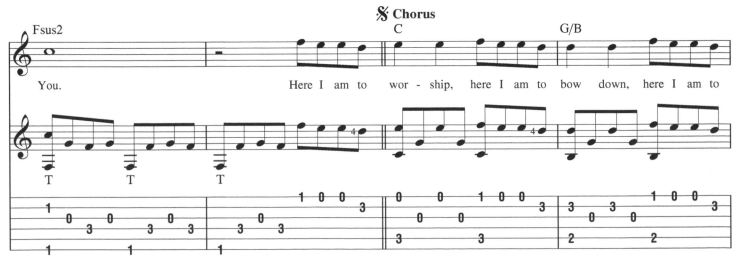

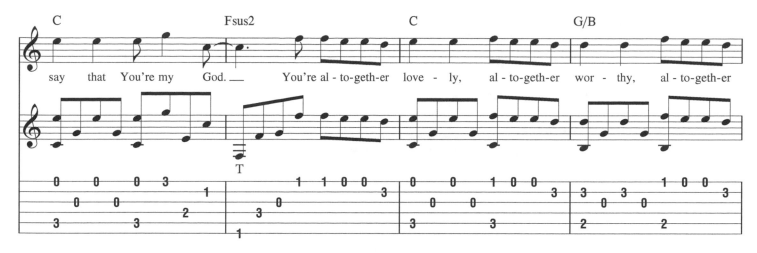

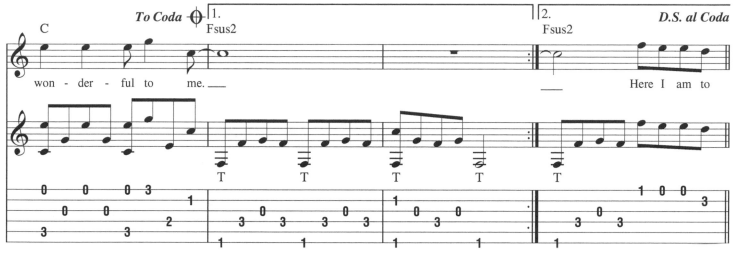

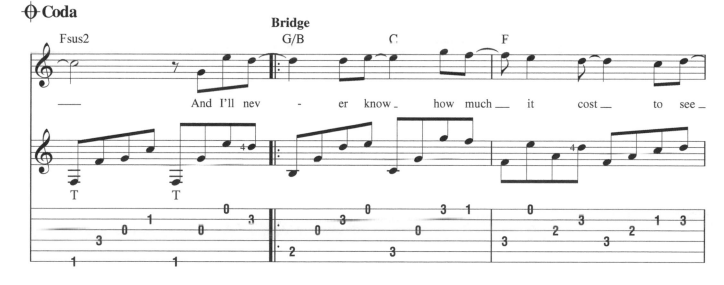

Chorus

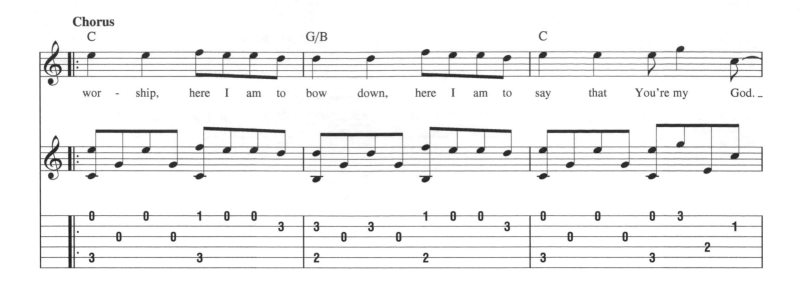

wor - ship, here I am to bow down, here I am to say that You're my God.

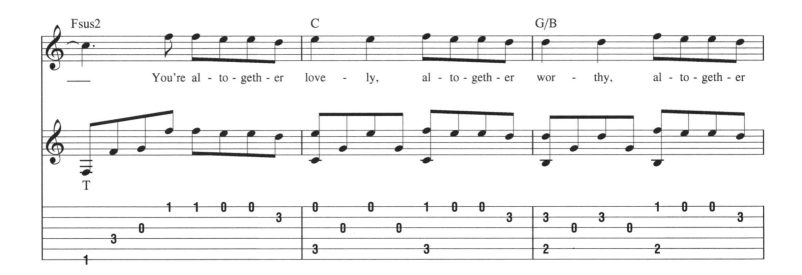

You're al - to - geth - er love - ly, al - to - geth - er wor - thy, al - to - geth - er

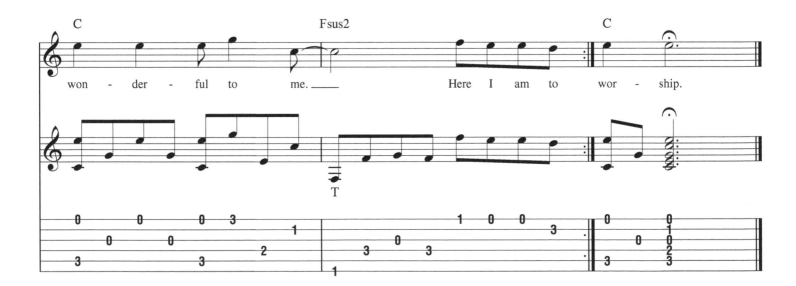

won - der - ful to me. Here I am to wor - ship.

Additional Lyrics

2. King of all days, oh, so highly exalted,
Glorious in heaven above.
Humbly You came to the earth You created,
All for love's sake became poor.

His Eye Is on the Sparrow

Words by Civilla D. Martin
Music by Charles H. Gabriel

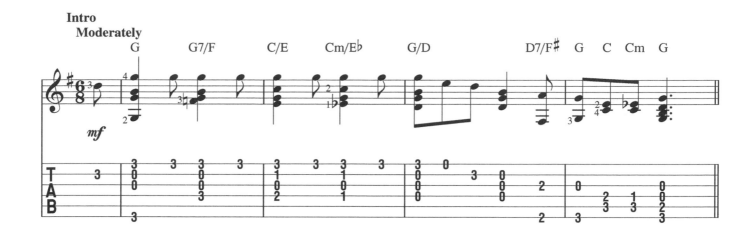

1. Why should I feel dis - cour - aged? _____ Why should the shad - ows
2. Let not your heart be troub - led. _____ His ten - der word I
3. *See additional lyrics*

come? Why should my heart be lone - ly, _____
hear. And rest - ing on His good - ness, _____

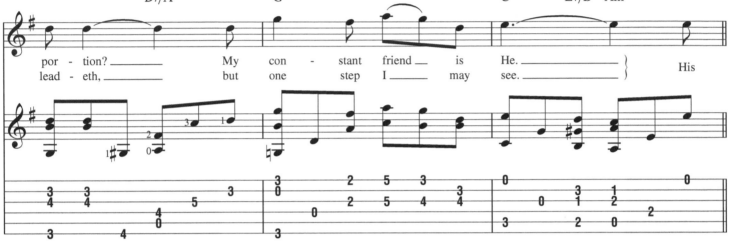

Chorus

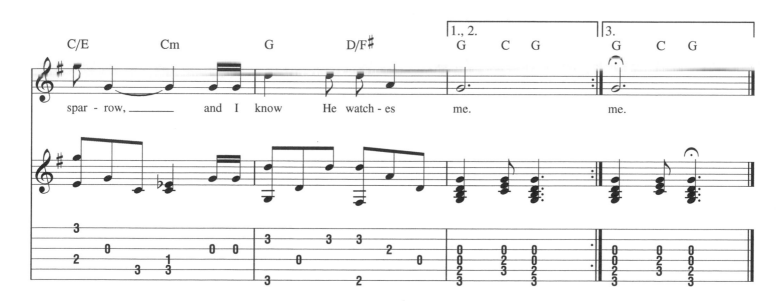

Additional Lyrics

3. Whenever I am tempted, whenever clouds arise,
When song gives place to sighing, when hope within me dies.
I draw the closer to Him, from care He sets me free.

Holy, Holy, Holy

Words by Reginald Heber
Music by John B. Dykes

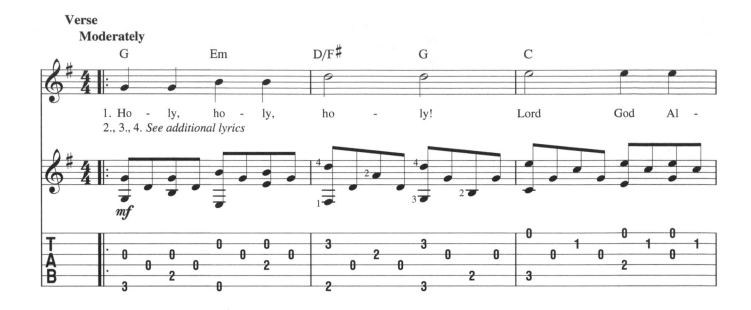

Verse
Moderately

1. Ho - ly, ho - ly, ho - ly! Lord God Al -
2., 3., 4. *See additional lyrics*

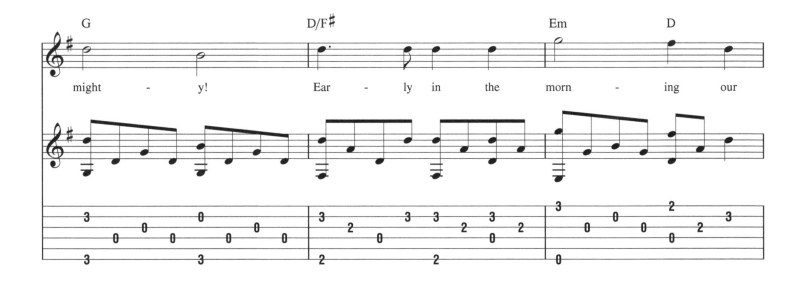

might - y! Ear - ly in the morn - ing our

songs shall rise to Thee. Ho - ly, ho - ly,

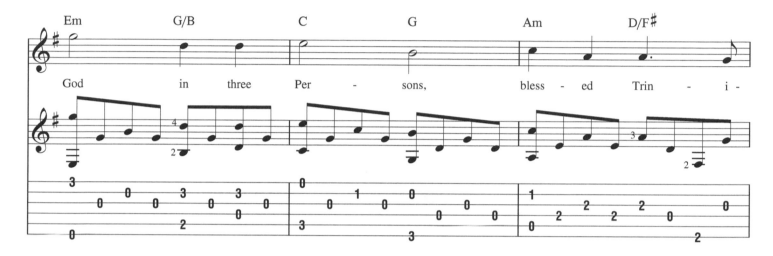

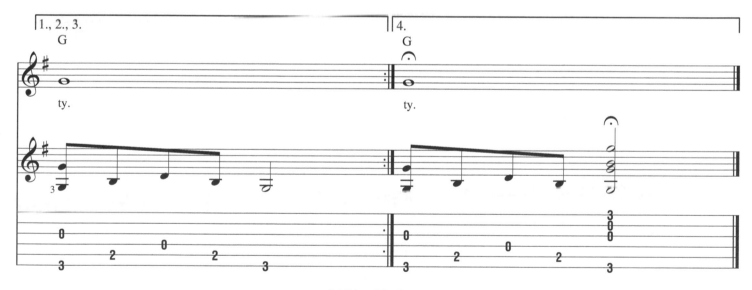

Additional Lyrics

2. Holy, holy, holy! All the saints adore Thee,
   Casting down their golden crowns around the glassy sea;
   Cherubim and seraphim falling down before Thee,
   Which wert and art and evermore shalt be.

3. Holy, holy, holy! Though the darkness hide Thee,
   Though the eye of sinful man Thy glory may not see.
   Only Thou art holy; there is none beside Thee,
   Perfect in power, in love, and purity.

4. Holy, holy, holy! Lord God Almighty!
   All Thy works shall praise Thy name in earth and sky and sea.
   Holy, holy, holy, merciful and mighty!
   God in three Persons, blessed Trinity!

How Great Is Our God

Words and Music by Chris Tomlin, Jesse Reeves and Ed Cash

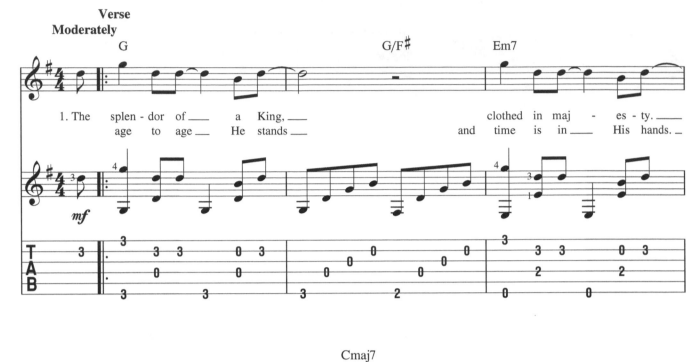

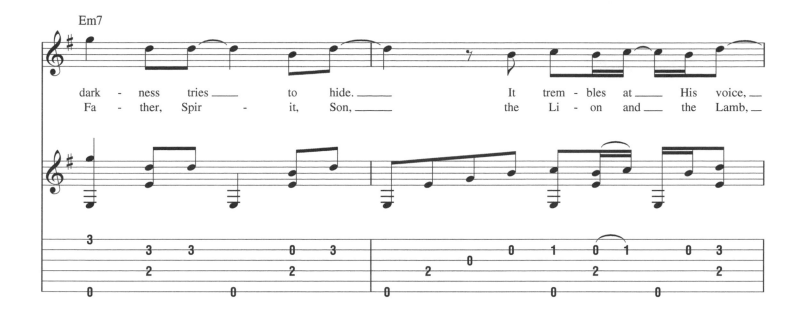

Chorus

praise. My heart will sing, — "How great   is our

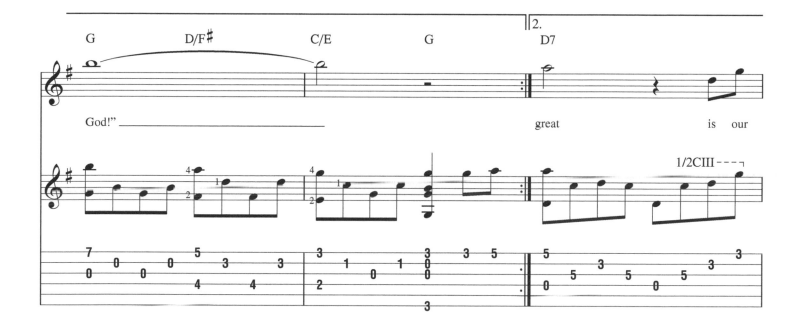

God!" _____ great   is our

God!"   How great ___

Outro-Chorus

Indescribable

Words and Music by Laura Story and Jesse Reeves

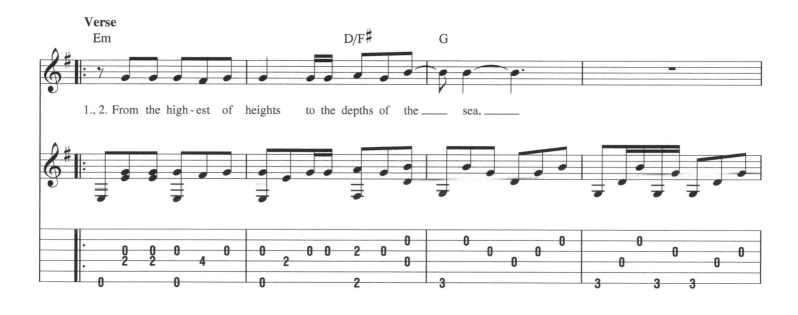

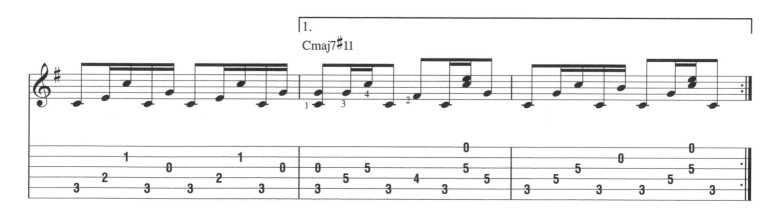

Bridge

You are a - maz - ing ___ God. ___

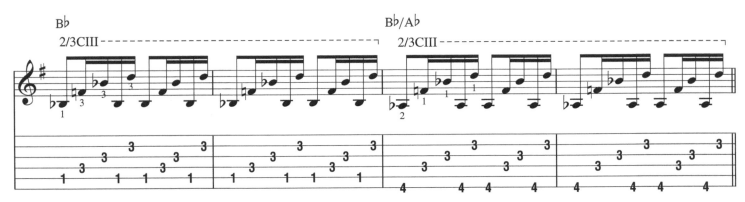

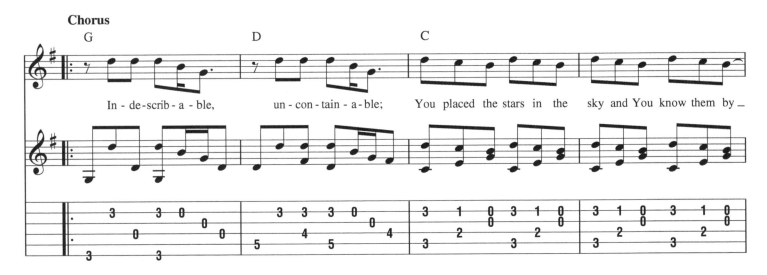

Chorus

In - de - scrib - a - ble, un - con - tain - a - ble; You placed the stars in the sky and You know them by ___

___ name. ___ You are a - maz - ing, ___ God. ___

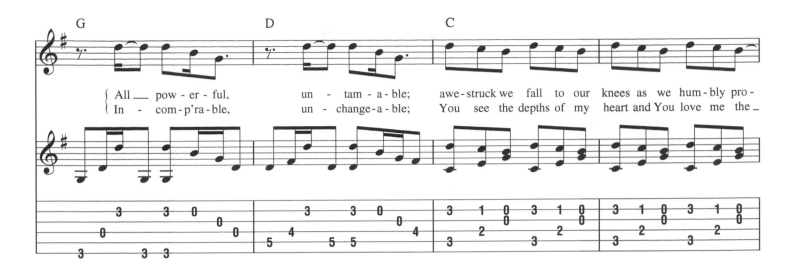

All — pow-er-ful, un - tam-a-ble; awe-struck we fall to our knees as we hum-bly pro-
In - com-p'ra-ble, un - change-a-ble; You see the depths of my heart and You love me the —

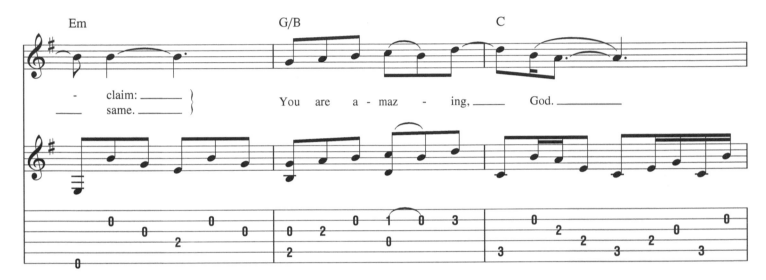

-claim: ____
____ same. ____

You are a - maz - ing, ____ God. ____

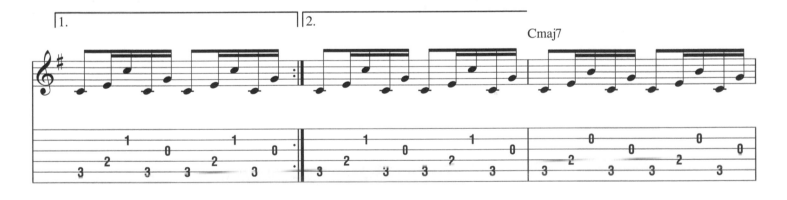

1.   2.   Cmaj7

You are a - maz - ing, ____ God. ____

rit.

In the Garden

Words and Music by C. Austin Miles

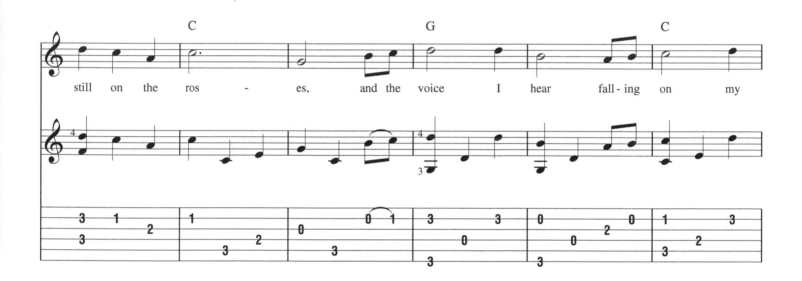

Chorus

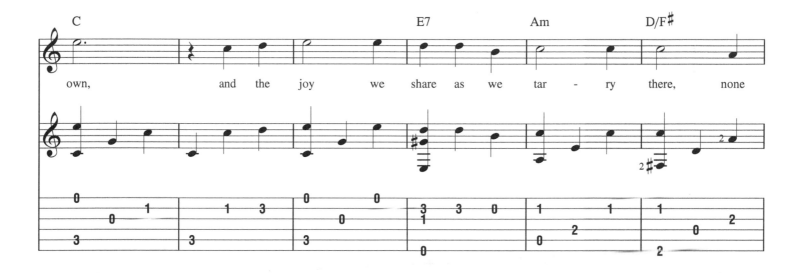

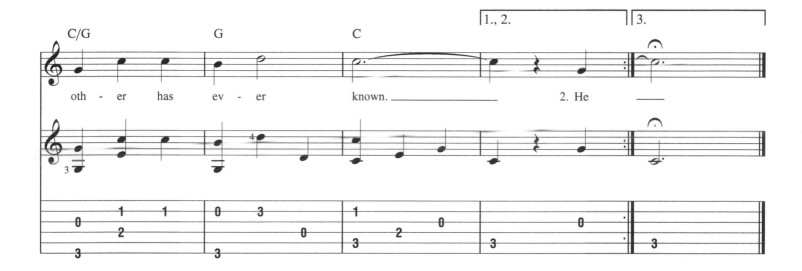

Additional Lyrics

2. He speaks, and the sound of His voice
   Is so sweet the birds hush their singing,
   And the melody that He gave to me
   Within my heart is ringing.

3. I'd stay in the garden with Him
   Though the night around me be falling,
   But He bids me go; through the voice of woe
   His voice to me is calling.

Joyful, Joyful, We Adore Thee

Words by Henry van Dyke
Music by Ludwig van Beethoven, melody from *Ninth Symphony*
Adapted by Edward Hodges

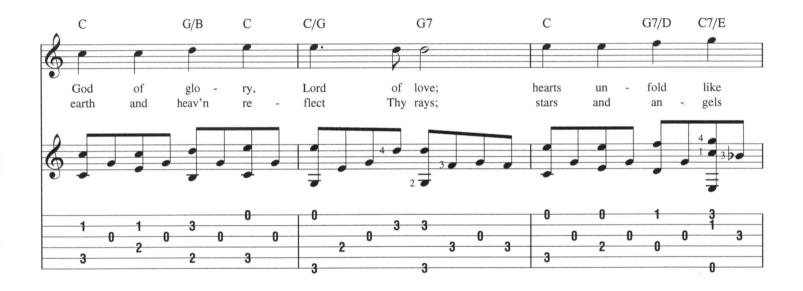

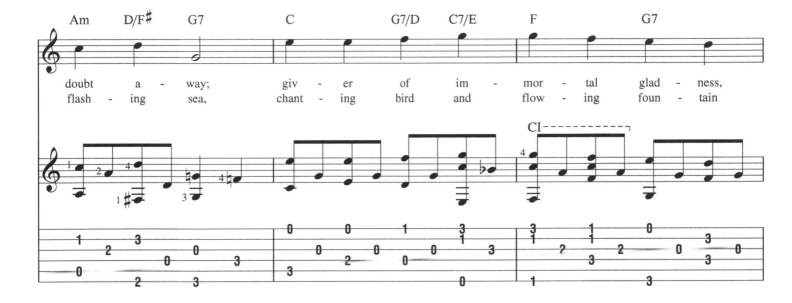

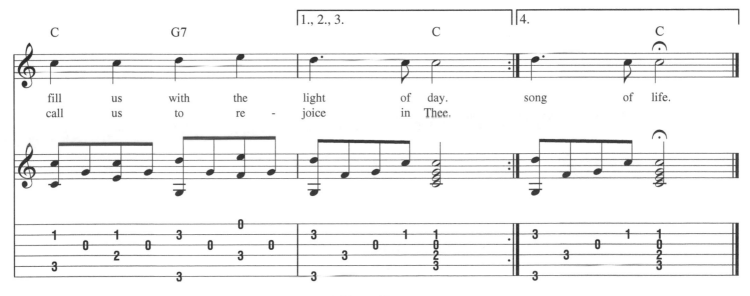

Additional Lyrics

3. Thou art giving and forgiving,
   Ever blessing, ever blest,
   Wellspring of the joy of living,
   Ocean depth of happy rest!
   Thou our Father, Christ our Brother;
   All who live in love are Thine.
   Teach us how to love each other,
   Lift us to the joy divine.

4. Mortals, join the happy chorus
   Which the morning stars began;
   Father love is reigning o'er us,
   Brother love binds man to man.
   Ever singing, march we onward,
   Victors in the midst of strife;
   Joyful music leads us sunward
   In the triumph song of life.

My Faith Looks Up to Thee

Words by Ray Palmer
Music by Lowell Mason

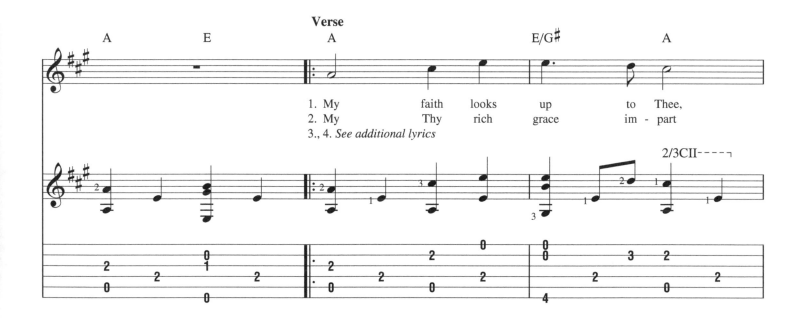

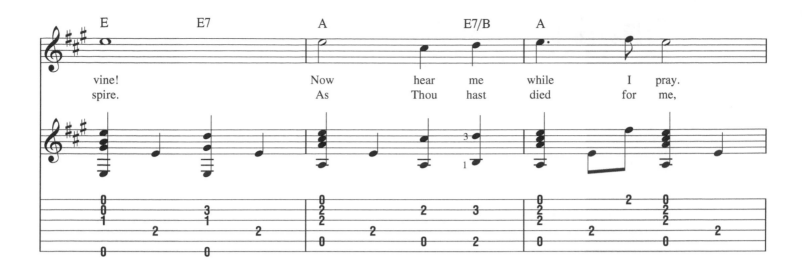

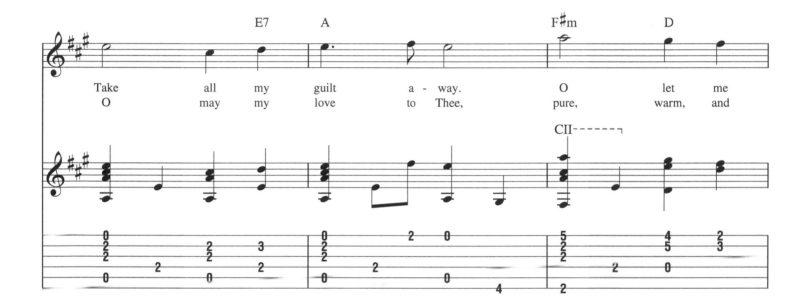

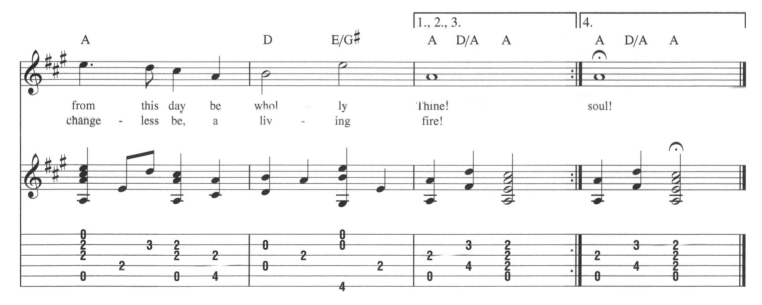

Additional Lyrics

3. While life's dark maze I tread
   And griefs around me spread,
   Be Thou my guide;
   Bid darkness turn to day,
   Wipe sorrow's tears away,
   Nor let me ever stray from Thee aside.

4. When ends life's passing dream,
   When death's cold, threat'ning stream
   Shall o'er me roll,
   Blest Savior, then, in love,
   Fear and distrust remove;
   O lift me safe above, a ransomed soul!

Shall We Gather at the River?

Words and Music by Robert Lowry

Chorus

Yes, we'll gath - er at the riv - er, the beau - ti - ful, the beau - ti - ful ____

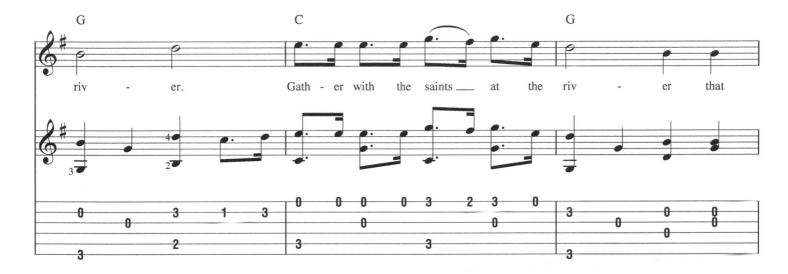

riv - er. Gath - er with the saints ___ at the riv - er that

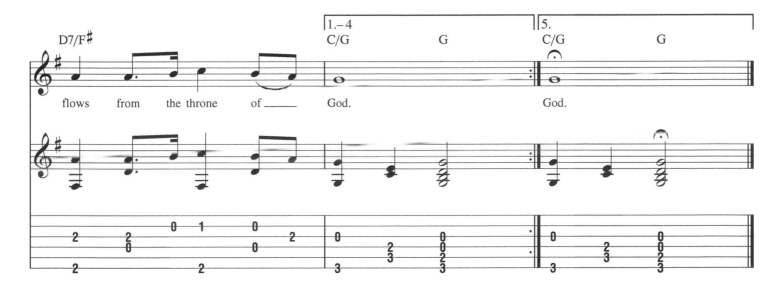

flows from the throne of ____ God. God.

Additional Lyrics

2. On the margin of the river,
   Washing up its silver spray,
   We shall walk and worship ever,
   All the happy, golden day.

3. On the bosom of the river,
   Where the Savior King we own,
   We shall meet and sorrow never
   'Neath the glory of the throne.

4. Ere we reach the shining river,
   Lay we ev'ry burden down;
   Grace our spirits will deliver
   And provide a robe and crown.

5. Soon we'll reach the shining river,
   Soon our pilgrimage will cease.
   Soon our happy hearts will quiver
   With the melody of peace.

There Is a Redeemer

Words and Music by Melody Green

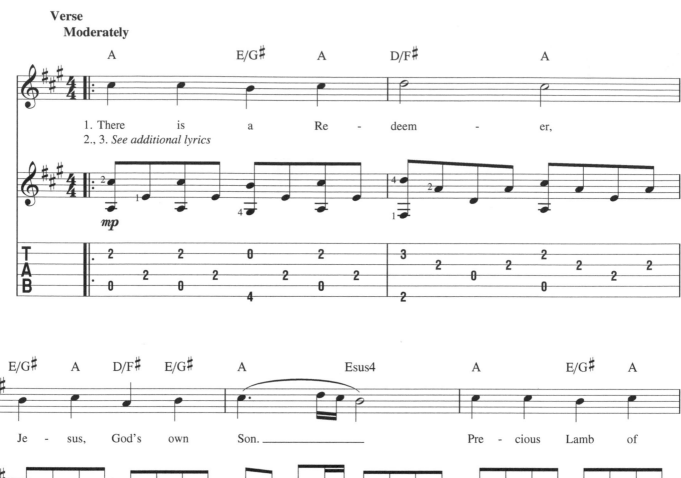

1. There is a Re - deem - er,
2., 3. *See additional lyrics*

Je - sus, God's own Son. _____ Pre - cious Lamb of

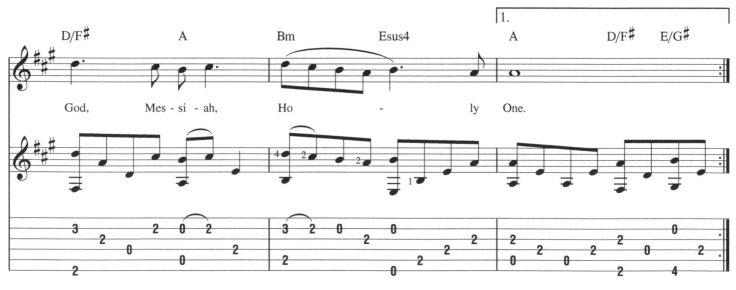

God, Mes - si - ah, Ho - ly One.

Chorus

One.   Thank You, oh, my Fa - ther, for

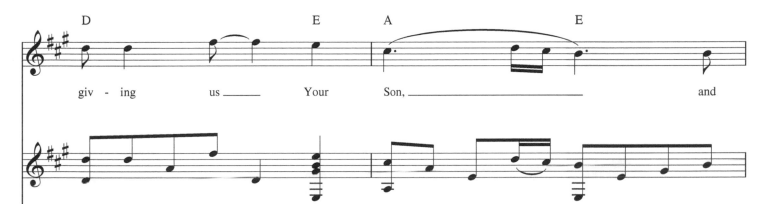

giv - ing us Your Son, and

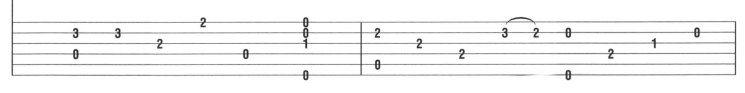

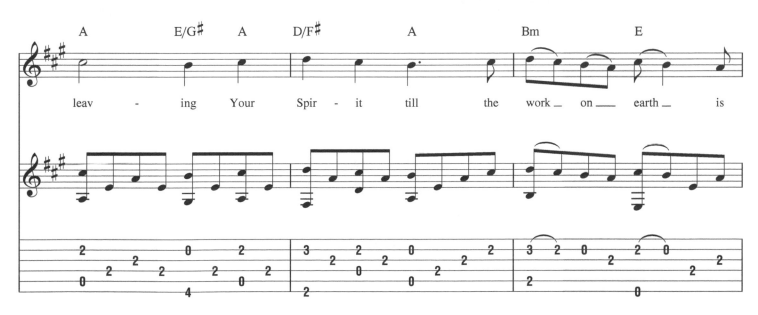

leav - ing Your Spir - it till the work on earth is

done,   and   leav - ing   Your   Spir - it   till   the

work __ on __ earth __ is   done.

Additional Lyrics

2. Jesus, my Redeemer,
   Name above all names,
   Precious Lamb of God, Messiah,
   Oh, for sinners slain.

3. When I stand in glory,
   I will see His face,
   And there I'll serve my King forever
   In that holy place.

Shout to the Lord

Words and Music by Darlene Zschech

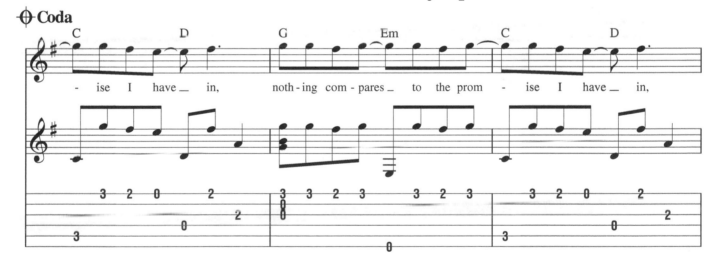

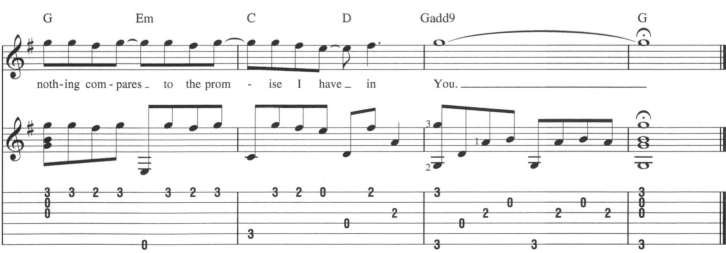

This Is My Father's World

Words by Maltbie D. Babcock
Music by Franklin L. Sheppard

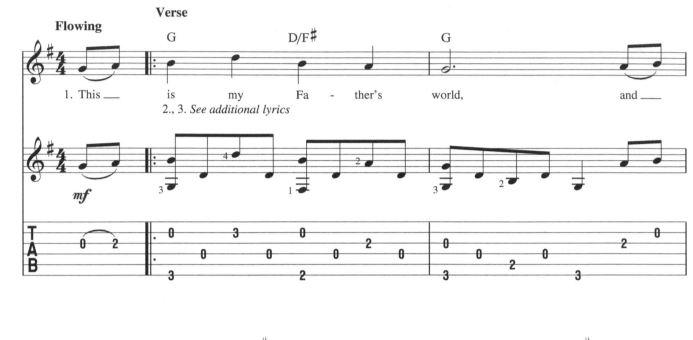

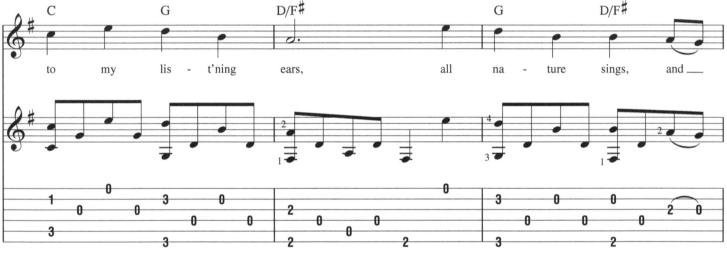

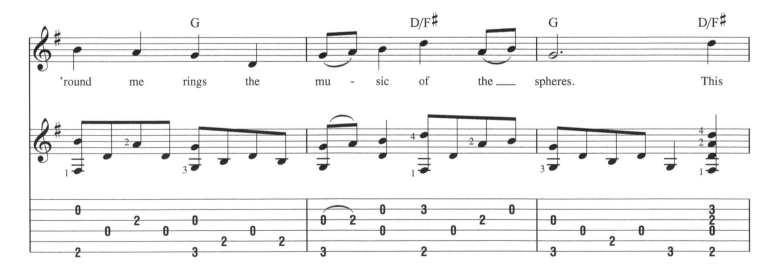

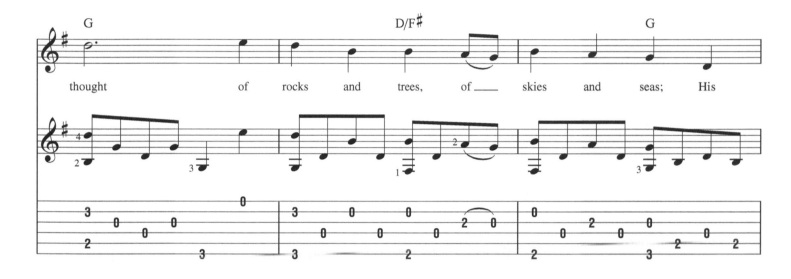

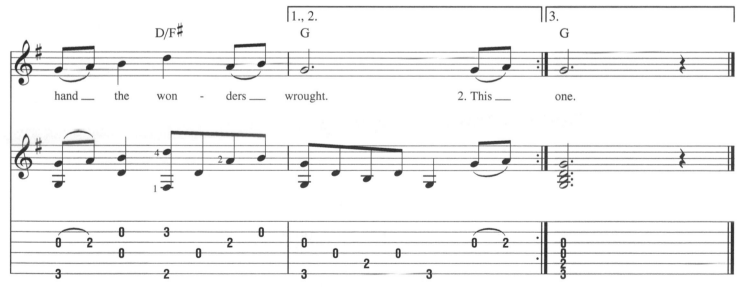

Additional Lyrics

2. This is my Father's world.
   The birds their carols raise,
   The morning light, the lily white,
   Declare their maker's praise.
   This is my Father's world.
   He shines in all that's fair;
   In the rustling grass I hear Him pass,
   He speaks to me ev'rywhere.

3. This is my Father's world.
   O let me ne'er forget
   That though the wrong seems oft so strong,
   God is the Ruler yet.
   This is my Father's world,
   The battle is not done;
   Jesus who died shall be satisfied,
   And earth and heav'n be one.

Turn Your Eyes Upon Jesus

Words and Music by Helen H. Lemmel

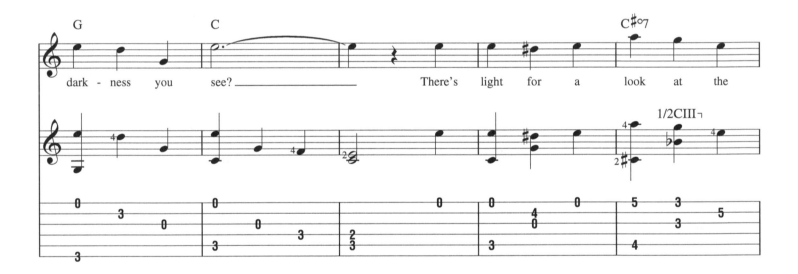

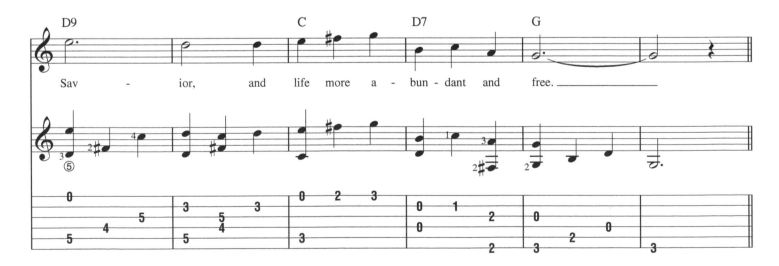

Chorus

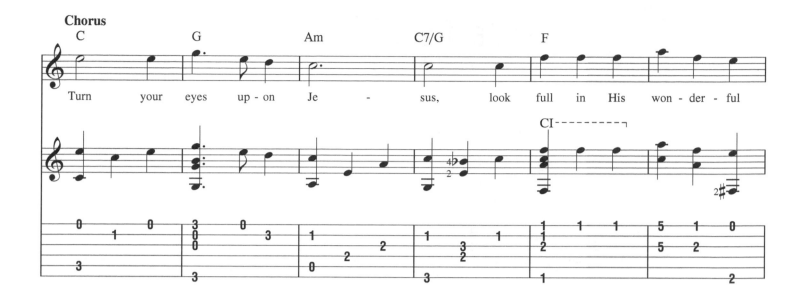

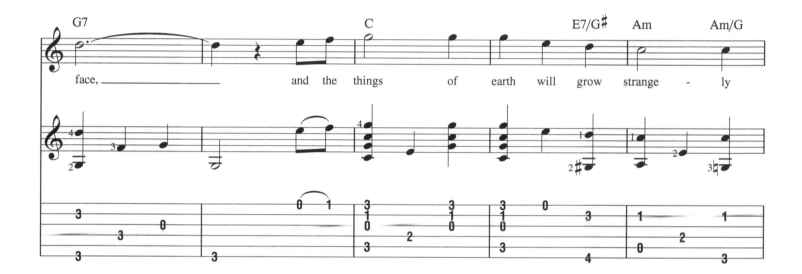

Additional Lyrics

2. Through death into life everlasting
   He passed, and we follow Him there;
   O'er us sin no more hath dominion
   For more than conquerors we are!

3. His word shall not fail you He promised;
   Believe Him, and all will be well.
   Then go to a world that is dying,
   His perfect salvation to tell!

We Fall Down

Words and Music by Chris Tomlin

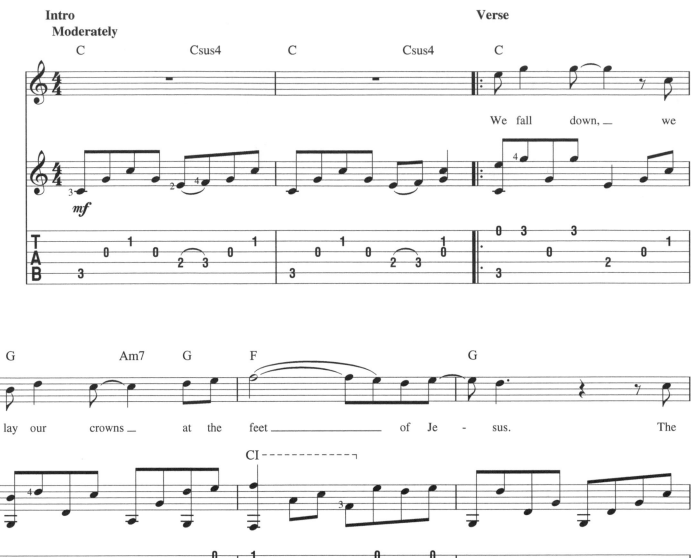

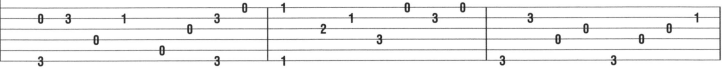

Chorus

"Ho - ly, ho - ly, ho - ly." We cry, "Ho - ly, ho - ly, ho - ly." We cry,

"Ho - ly, ho - ly, ho - ly is the Lamb."

Outro

"Ho - ly, ho - ly, ho - ly is the Lamb."

What a Friend We Have in Jesus

Words by Joseph M. Scriven
Music by Charles C. Converse

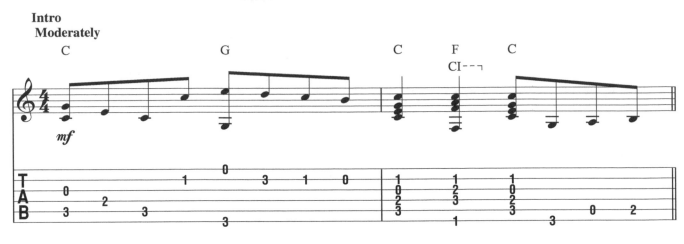

1. What a friend we have in Je - sus, all our sins and griefs to
2., 3. *See additional lyrics*

bear. What a priv - i - lege to car - ry

Additional Lyrics

2. Have we trials and temptations?
   Is there trouble anywhere?
   We should never be discouraged;
   Take it to the Lord in prayer.
   Can we find a friend so faithful
   Who will all our sorrows share?
   Jesus knows our ev'ry weakness;
   Take it to the Lord in prayer.

3. Are we weak and heavy-laden,
   Cumbered with a load of care?
   Precious Savior, still our refuge;
   Take it to the Lord in prayer.
   Do thy friends despise, forsake thee?
   Take it to the Lord in prayer.
   In His arms He'll take and shield thee;
   Thou wilt find a solace there.

Worthy Is the Lamb

Words and Music by Darlene Zschech

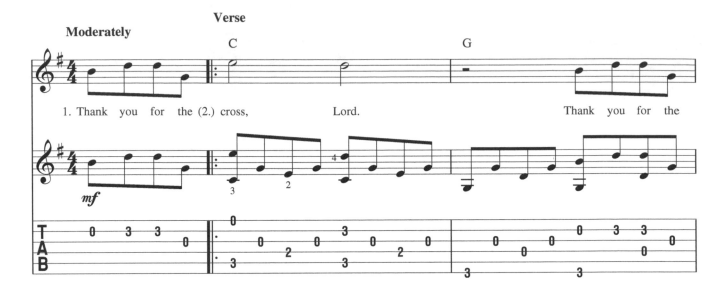

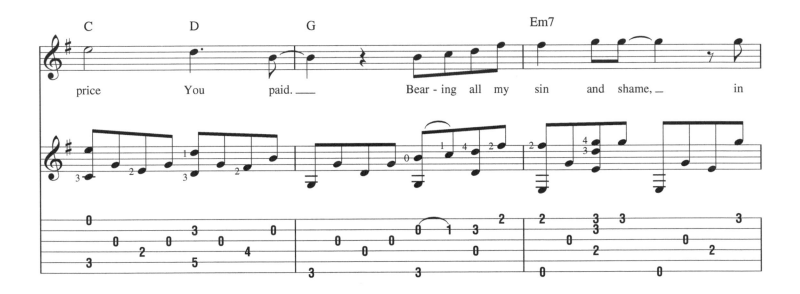

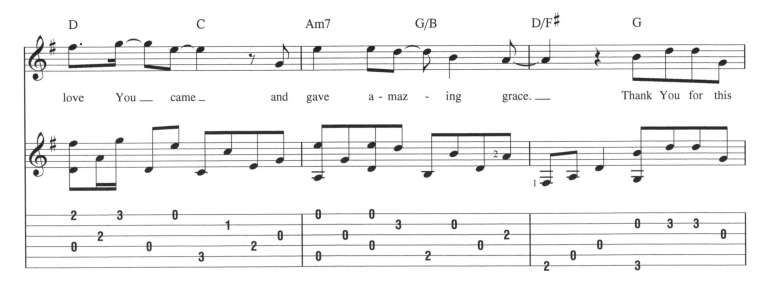

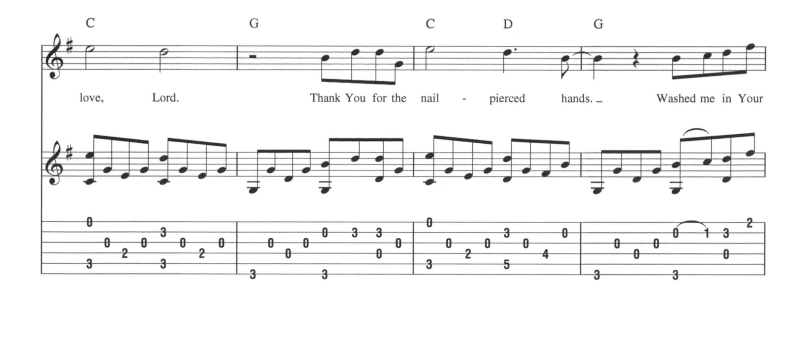

love, Lord. Thank You for the nail - pierced hands. _ Washed me in Your

cleans - ing flow, _ now all I _ know, _ Your for - give - ness and _ em - brace. _

% Chorus

Wor - thy is _ the Lamb, _ seat - ed on _ the throne. _

Crown You now with man - y crowns, You reign vic - to - ri - ous.

High and lift - ed up, Je - sus, Son of God. The

*Dar - ling of heav - en cru - ci - fied. Wor - thy is the

*Alternate lyric: Treasure

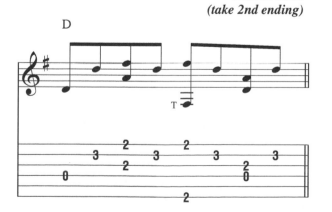

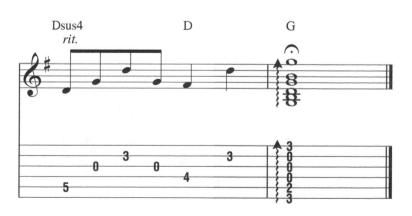

FINGERPICKING GUITAR BOOKS

Hone your fingerpicking skills with these great songbooks featuring solo guitar arrangements in standard notation and tablature. The arrangements in these books are carefully written for intermediate-level guitarists. Each song combines melody and harmony in one superb guitar fingerpicking arrangement. Each book also includes an introduction to basic fingerstyle guitar.

 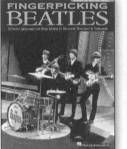 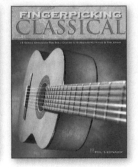   

Fingerpicking Acoustic
00699614 15 songs......................$14.99

Fingerpicking Acoustic Classics
00160211 15 songs......................$16.99

Fingerpicking Acoustic Hits
00160202 15 songs......................$12.99

Fingerpicking Acoustic Rock
00699764 14 songs......................$16.99

Fingerpicking Ballads
00699717 15 songs......................$15.99

Fingerpicking Beatles
00699049 30 songs......................$24.99

Fingerpicking Beethoven
00702390 15 pieces......................$10.99

Fingerpicking Blues
00701277 15 songs......................$12.99

Fingerpicking Broadway Favorites
00699843 15 songs......................$9.99

Fingerpicking Broadway Hits
00699838 15 songs......................$7.99

Fingerpicking Campfire
00275964 15 songs......................$14.99

Fingerpicking Celtic Folk
00701148 15 songs......................$12.99

Fingerpicking Children's Songs
00699712 15 songs......................$9.99

Fingerpicking Christian
00701076 15 songs......................$12.99

Fingerpicking Christmas
00699599 20 carols......................$12.99

Fingerpicking Christmas Classics
00701695 15 songs......................$7.99

Fingerpicking Christmas Songs
00171333 15 songs......................$10.99

Fingerpicking Classical
00699620 15 pieces......................$10.99

Fingerpicking Country
00699687 17 songs......................$12.99

Fingerpicking Disney
00699711 15 songs......................$17.99

Fingerpicking Early Jazz Standards
00276565 15 songs $12.99

Fingerpicking Duke Ellington
00699845 15 songs......................$9.99

Fingerpicking Enya
00701161 15 songs......................$16.99

Fingerpicking Film Score Music
00160143 15 songs......................$12.99

Fingerpicking Gospel
00701059 15 songs......................$9.99

Fingerpicking Hit Songs
00160195 15 songs......................$12.99

Fingerpicking Hymns
00699688 15 hymns $12.99

Fingerpicking Irish Songs
00701965 15 songs......................$10.99

Fingerpicking Italian Songs
00159778 15 songs......................$12.99

Fingerpicking Jazz Favorites
00699844 15 songs......................$12.99

Fingerpicking Jazz Standards
00699840 15 songs......................$12.99

Fingerpicking Elton John
00237495 15 songs......................$15.99

Fingerpicking Latin Favorites
00699842 15 songs......................$12.99

Fingerpicking Latin Standards
00699837 15 songs......................$17.99

Fingerpicking Andrew Lloyd Webber
00699839 14 songs......................$16.99

Fingerpicking Love Songs
00699841 15 songs......................$14.99

Fingerpicking Love Standards
00699836 15 songs $9.99

Fingerpicking Lullabyes
00701276 16 songs......................$9.99

Fingerpicking Movie Music
00699919 15 songs......................$14.99

Fingerpicking Mozart
00699794 15 pieces......................$10.99

Fingerpicking Pop
00699615 15 songs......................$14.99

Fingerpicking Popular Hits
00139079 14 songs......................$12.99

Fingerpicking Praise
00699714 15 songs......................$14.99

Fingerpicking Rock
00699716 15 songs......................$14.99

Fingerpicking Standards
00699613 17 songs......................$15.99

Fingerpicking Wedding
00699637 15 songs......................$10.99

Fingerpicking Worship
00700554 15 songs......................$14.99

Fingerpicking Neil Young – Greatest Hits
00700134 16 songs......................$17.99

Fingerpicking Yuletide
00699654 16 songs......................$12.99

HAL•LEONARD®

Order these and more great publications from your favorite music retailer at
halleonard.com

Prices, contents and availability subject to change without notice.

 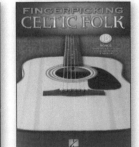   

christian guitar songbooks

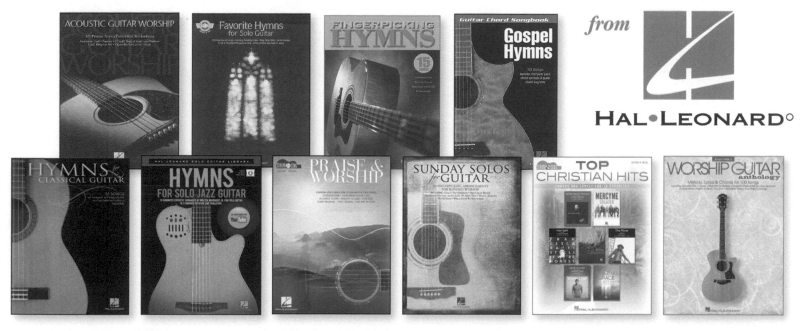

from **HAL•LEONARD®**

ACOUSTIC GUITAR WORSHIP

30 praise song favorites arranged for guitar, including: Awesome God • Forever • I Could Sing of Your Love Forever • Lord, Reign in Me • Open the Eyes of My Heart • and more.
00699672 Solo Guitar.. $14.99

FAVORITE HYMNS FOR SOLO GUITAR

Amazing Grace • Christ the Lord Is Risen Today • For the Beauty of the Earth • Holy, Holy, Holy • In the Garden • Let Us Break Bread Together • O for a Thousand Tongues to Sing • Were You There? • What a Friend We Have in Jesus • When I Survey the Wondrous Cross • more.
00699275 Fingerstyle Guitar $12.99

FINGERPICKING HYMNS

Abide with Me • Amazing Grace • Beneath the Cross of Jesus • Come, Thou Fount of Every Blessing • For the Beauty of the Earth • A Mighty Fortress Is Our God • Rock of Ages • and more.
00699688 Solo Guitar.................................... $9.99

FINGERPICKING WORSHIP

Agnus Dei • Amazing Grace (My Chains Are Gone) • How Deep the Father's Love for Us • How Great Is Our God • I Worship You, Almighty God • More Precious Than Silver • There Is a Redeemer • We Fall Down • and more, plus an easy introduction to basic fingerstyle guitar.
00700554 Solo Guitar.................................... $10.99

GOSPEL GUITAR SONGBOOK

Includes notes & tab for fingerpicking and Travis picking arrangements of 15 favorites: Amazing Grace • Blessed Assurance • Do Lord • I've Got Peace Like a River • Just a Closer Walk with Thee • O Happy Day • Precious Memories • Rock of Ages • Swing Low, Sweet Chariot • There Is Power in the Blood • When the Saints Go Marching In • and more!
00695372 Guitar with Notes & Tab $9.95

GOSPEL HYMNS

Amazing Grace • At the Cross • Blessed Assurance • Higher Ground • I've Got Peace like a River • In the Garden • Love Lifted Me • The Old Rugged Cross • Rock of Ages • What a Friend We Have in Jesus • When the Saints Go Marching In • Wondrous Love • and more.
00700463
Lyrics/Chord Symbols/Guitar Chord Diagrams........ $14.99

HYMNS FOR CLASSICAL GUITAR

Amazing Grace • Be Thou My Vision • Come, Thou Fount of Every Blessing • For the Beauty of the Earth • Joyful, Joyful, We Adore Thee • My Faith Looks up to Thee • Rock of Ages • What a Friend We Have in Jesus • and more.
00701898 Solo Guitar.................................... $14.99

HYMNS FOR SOLO JAZZ GUITAR

Book/Online Video

Abide with Me • Amazing Grace • Blessed Assurance • God Is So Good • Just a Closer Walk with Thee • Londonderry Air • Oh How I Love Jesus • Softly and Tenderly • Sweet Hour of Prayer • What a Friend We Have in Jesus.
00153842 Solo Guitar.................................... $19.99

MODERN WORSHIP – GUITAR CHORD SONGBOOK

Amazed • Amazing Grace (My Chains Are Gone) • At the Cross • Beautiful One • Everlasting God • How Can I Keep from Singing • I Am Free • Let God Arise • Let My Words Be Few (I'll Stand in Awe of You) • Made to Worship • Mighty to Save • Nothing but the Blood • Offering • Sing to the King • Today Is the Day • Your Name • and more.
00701801
Lyrics/Chord Symbols/Guitar Chord Diagrams........ $16.99

PRAISE & WORSHIP – STRUM & SING

This inspirational collection features 25 favorites for guitarists to strum and sing. Includes chords and lyrics for: Amazing Grace (My Chains Are Gone) • Cornerstone • Everlasting God • Forever • The Heart of Worship • How Great Is Our God • In Christ Alone • Mighty to Save • 10,000 Reasons (Bless the Lord) • This I Believe • We Fall Down • and more.
00152381 Guitar/Vocal $12.99

SACRED SONGS FOR CLASSICAL GUITAR

Bind Us Together • El Shaddai • Here I Am, Lord • His Name Is Wonderful • How Great Thou Art • I Walked Today Where Jesus Walked • On Eagle's Wings • Thou Art Worthy • and more.
00702426 Guitar.. $14.99

SUNDAY SOLOS FOR GUITAR

Great Is Thy Faithfulness • Here I Am to Worship • How Great Is Our God • Joyful, Joyful, We Adore Thee • There Is a Redeemer • We Fall Down • What a Friend We Have in Jesus • and more!
00703083 Guitar.. $14.99

TOP CHRISTIAN HITS – STRUM & SING GUITAR

Good Good Father (Chris Tomlin) • Greater (MercyMe) • Holy Spirit (Francesca Battistelli) • I Am (Crowder) • Same Power (Jeremy Camp) • This Is Amazing Grace (Phil Wickham) • and more.
00156331 Guitar/Vocal $12.99

THE WORSHIP GUITAR ANTHOLOGY – VOLUME 1

This collection contains melody, lyrics & chords for 100 contemporary favorites, such as: Beautiful One • Forever • Here I Am to Worship • Hosanna (Praise Is Rising) • How He Loves • In Christ Alone • Mighty to Save • Our God • Revelation Song • Your Grace Is Enough • and dozens more.
00101864 Melody/Lyrics/Chords.......................... $16.99

WORSHIP SOLOS FOR FINGERSTYLE GUITAR

Ancient Words • Before the Throne of God Above • Broken Vessels (Amazing Grace) • Cornerstone • Good Good Father • Great Are You Lord • Holy Spirit • I Will Rise • King of My Heart • Lord, I Need You • O Come to the Altar • O Praise the Name (Anastasis) • Oceans (Where Feet May Fail) • 10,000 Reasons (Bless the Lord) • Your Name.
00276831 Guitar.. $14.99

TOP WORSHIP SONGS FOR GUITAR

Amazing Grace (My Chains Are Gone) • Because He Lives, Amen • Cornerstone • Forever (We Sing Hallelujah) • Good Good Father • Holy Spirit • Jesus Messiah • Lead Me to the Cross • Our God • Revelation Song • This Is Amazing Grace • We Believe • Your Grace Is Enough • and more.
00160854 Melody/Lyrics/Chords.......................... $12.99

Prices, contents and availability subject to change without notice.

FOR MORE INFORMATION,
SEE YOUR LOCAL MUSIC DEALER,
OR WRITE TO:

HAL•LEONARD®

7777 W. BLUEMOUND RD. P.O. BOX 13819
MILWAUKEE, WISCONSIN 53213

www.halleonard.com